FALLING UP

a guide for nervous mediums

DENISE LITCHFIELD

Copyright © 2020 by Denise Litchfield

All rights reserved.
No part of this publication may be reproduced, stored in a retrieval system, or transmitted in any form or by any means, electronic, mechanical, photocopying, recording, scanning, or otherwise, without the prior written permission of the author.

Editing by Tia Ross
Book design by DTPerfect.com
Front cover photo by Lisa Fotios from Pexels

ISBN (paperback) 978-0-646-82883-1
ISBN (ebook) 978-0-6450737-0-6

CONTENTS

Introduction. vii

1. The first time I fell up 1
2. Don't just do something; sit there 9
3. Today's downward dog 15
4. It might feel like falling down instead of up 21
5. One-minute ways to fall up. 25
6. When it really sucks 29
7. A list to help you know you've fallen up. 33

Resources 37
About the author. 39

DEDICATION

To Paul Jacobs, whose teachings and stories
helped me to see God in an orange.

INTRODUCTION

This is a tiny book for new psychic mediums and anyone curious about spirit. Its goal is to help you loosen the grip on this world in order to feel the next one.

As a curious new psychic or medium, the unseen world might seem out of reach or even unreal. In fact, you're not even sure there is one, but there are odd and vivid times when connection to the next world happened. It felt wonderful, like a hug from your favourite grandmother, and you remember the feeling even now.

Having one foot in this world and one in the next (like you already have) is a natural state where we allow the spirit world to take the lead so we can truly be a phone line between the worlds. You've already felt what it's like to fall up and you want more.

Yes, you already have one foot in the next world.

You might be a shy introvert who loves alone time. Days drift by without leaving the house. Cups of tea go cold around a home strewn with creative projects, and yoga pants are for day wear as well as on the mat.

You love daydreaming and had imaginary friends. Your best buddy might have been a dog or the creek down the hill, rather than a living human. This is all part of falling up and you already recognise it because connecting to the next world came naturally as a child.

Introduction

Congratulations, you're a medium. A real medium, not the sideshow clowns with turbans tracing palms and removing curses.

You're a medium in a quiet Mom-and-Pop kind of way because you've always been, but perhaps never realised 'til right now.

From goosebumpy shivers to inner visions like the movies, you're oh so curious. A beloved someone might already be in the next world, and you're wondering how to get a message through.

Being a medium means lots of falling down while exploring how to get messages through and be accurate as well as uplifting.

But there's another side of mediumship that can never be taught.

No weekend workshop or expensive guru can teach this other side because it's discovered within. I call it falling up.

Falling up has many names. Grace could be one. Surrender could be another. Falling up is less about crushed velvet turbans and crystals and more about a deep inner belonging to something greater, however that 'something greater' is understood.

This tiny book will help you fall up with short stories, easy mini exercises and inspiration. It will keep your feet walking the long trail of the soul with minimum blisters until you arrive in the arms of your own 'something greater.'

May you find spirit right where you are.

THE FIRST TIME I FELL UP

"You are a child of the universe no less than the trees and the stars; you have a right to be here."

—Max Ehrmann, 1927, Desiderata

One Christmas, my family squeezed into a mint green VW beetle for a three-day drive to the Gold Coast. My head rested on a giant panda I crammed in and radio range was long gone.

Endless power lines looped by as the VW turtled along heat-hazed bitumen. In the monotony, I fell into a daydream.

With my bored nose pressed against the car window, everything suddenly felt connected. The power poles somehow knew the perfect distance to be apart, and red hills offered their bellies to the sun.

Everything seemed to breathe together and pulse with an awareness that also included me.

It was a dance mapped by an infinite choreographer in which every living thing knew its part. No magpie squawked out of sync and no sheep stumbled on its track.

For that moment, the world buzzed with a dazzling consciousness that I felt part of. I was a small skin-coloured thread woven into the universe's tapestry next to a black-and-white bear inside a mint green VW beetle.

I fell up.

There was a strange unity to everything seen from a little round car that day. For a tiny magical time, I understood the dance and knew the invisible steps.

It felt like every living thing danced in the steps of an invisible choreographer. Best of all, there could be no missteps. In this divine dance, everything fits and flows and we all know the moves.

Every bird knows the precise moment to join the great song, and every flower makes its appointment to bloom.

As soon as I was gone, I was back squeezed beside a giant panda on a hot highway with ordinary red hills and hours more driving till dark. For that small moment, I fell up and into the arms of spirit.

Falling up isn't a place, it's an attitude that can only be found inside. That's why even the biggest gurus and teachers can't teach it. Falling up is also hard. Falling up means letting go at a level that's scary for the fearful and scarier for the control freaks.

What it means to fall up

For a medium who wants to connect more to the spirit world, falling up is a leap into the arms of something greater than you to let the divine take the lead. It's allowing the blood back to knuckles gone white from holding on so long and baring your own belly to the sun.

Falling up has no spoiler alerts and no scripts. Like Christ's journey into the wilderness, we do it alone. When we return from our own wilderness, we have felt that kiss that can only be received from the unseen world, as Rumi says:

> "There is some kiss we want with our whole lives, the touch of spirit on the body. .....At night, I open the window and ask the moon to come and press its face against mine. Breathe into me. Close the language door and open the lovers window. The moon won't use the door, only the window."
>
> —Rumi

Later in the same year of the mint green VW trip, on a black and white TV with rounded edges and fake wood veneer, a movie helped me fall up again.

A wounded fighter pilot crashed to earth only to find himself traveling a light-filled escalator to heaven. But there was a mix up; he wasn't due to die for many years yet. The rest of the movie was set in the afterworld.

Something stirred

If the dance of the highway power poles was a taste that something greater was available, this old war movie hinted where that greater something might be.

From there it was a small jump to understanding the presences at night weren't just a fear of the dark, but a sensing of what was *in* the dark. Rather than Casper the Friendly Ghost, I recognised a benign influence like Glinda the North Witch.

My experience was not of separate individuals speaking to me as others report, but the presence of the spirit world as a whole that was with me as a child.

Now it's your turn:

In the last section I shared small private moments of awareness in daydreams or movie watching where the moving parade of life could be witnessed from a huge distance.

Where we are aware of being part of something greater and that our place in it is just as important. Now it's your turn.

Put down this book, rest the phone, and close the laptop. Gaze out of the window right here where you are.

Right now. All the devices will be there when you get back.

Looking back over your life, do you remember times when you, too, felt the magic, even for a second?

When something stirred, you felt an awareness all around you.

When was it?

How old were you?

What happened?

Go back and relive that moment. Chances are the memory will be vivid (that's spirit working right there).

Bonus gold stars for writing that experience in your journal. If you get stuck, remember falling up is easy. See where you can let go some more. If you're truly stuck, what makes you feel the magic again? There's a list below to spark imagination.

My list of magic:
(feel free to add your own)

- Watching my dog's paws as she dreams
- The smell of a baby
- The air after rain
- Your favourite childhood movie
- Nature films
- Songs sung in full voice in the car
- Facebook posts that bring tears in a good way
- Walking in the early morning before the world is awake
- Being near the ocean
- Seeing the moon rise
- Spooning with my partner after a good day

DON'T JUST DO SOMETHING; SIT THERE

"In the midst of movement and chaos, keep stillness inside of you."

—Anonymous

In the last section, we discovered private moments of magic by stepping back from the moving parade of life to witness it at a distance. By stepping back even for a moment, we feel a flicker of being in tandem with the great flow of life.

In these moments of grace we are gifted a preview of what being a medium is like. Most budding mediums either never get to this place or dash right past in search of more tools, tricks, and tips. Formal mediumship training is essential, but not 'til we discover ourselves first.

Mediums stand in the middle, literally between the worlds. To do that, space is required to step back from life and witness it at a calm distance. That space is hard won and usually filled with the kind of baggage that keeps coaches, healers, and therapists busy for years.

The promise of this is a tiny book is to help you loosen your grip on this world in order to feel the next one. Relax, knowing you aren't in control, and hand the steering wheel of your life over to spirit.

Take a seat; it's time to fall up

As a curious new psychic or medium, you may have heard about the need to meditate. You may have rolled your eyes at the thought of more meditation or squirmed through a mountain of guided recordings.

Falling up is a kind of meditation where we don't *do* anything except sit there. No fancy breathing or chants. No weird finger poses or pretzel shapes. No meeting wise men inside crystals or unicorns who talk through their third eye.

Falling up is stunningly simple: Just staying present with with eyes closed, letting thoughts flutter past like random butterflies.

Sitting in this way will grow to be peaceful and nourishing, and after a while, spirit may also join you. When they do, you have fallen up.

But sitting doing nothing is almost a crime these days. We're so busy, we forget to feel and be. Like the VW road trip, falling up is bathed in tiny moments of feeling. On the way, we meet ourselves and then the spirit world.

Another time I fell up

Four years into formal mediumship training, I still hadn't figured out what falling up was—partly because 'figuring out' required using the mind when the mind was supposed to be sitting still and not figuring anything.

But I did figure out this: I didn't like myself much.

Sitting in the golden draped sanctuary of the Arthur Findlay College (a real life Hogwarts for psychics and mediums), it was nearly showtime. My tutor was about to demonstrate mediumship. As all eyes closed for the opening prayer I felt the presence of the spirit world—not really surprising in a 365-room college devoted to the spirit arts.

Two presences at my elbows took me somewhere equally golden. I had the impression I was to 'meet' someone, although no words were spoken. Instantly, I felt this someone, who gazed at me with timeless eyes that knew every moment of my life, every sob, every joy, and lonely moment in my existence, and yet still loved me. The eyes saw it all:

- The kid who stole lollies from the local shop.
- The teenager who ran out on her fiancé.
- The underpaid jobs and failures of my life.

This spirit person took it all in giving forth an acceptance and all-encompassing compassion I'd never experienced before. I felt naked yet fully seen to the very soul as the gaze said, 'You are enough and you are loved.'

The meeting in the golden draped college sanctuary lasted seconds, like the VW Beetle moment. It was a tiny snapshot of touching the next world, leaving tears on my cheeks and a lightness in my heart.

I realised another important part of falling up; we meet ourselves through the lens of love.

Now it's your turn:

- Don't just do something; sit there.//
- Put down the book again.
- Close your eyes.
- Sit there.
- Repeat.
- *You can't mess this up.*

TODAY'S DOWNWARD DOG

"Don't wait to have it all figured out before sitting, you'll never get there. Sit your way towards it. Keep turning up. Sit your way there."

—MEDITATION TEACHER

A group of city social workers gathered disadvantaged and disinterested teens made callous by life in order to teach them something.

Week after week, the teenagers failed to make the set outcome of the class. At first, the social workers were disappointed and heartbroken. Life had yet again failed these kids and left them with hardened eyes and hopeless hearts.

Yet week after week the kids turned up.

The social workers noticed something. Whatever their look-good-on-a-report goal was, something else was happening.

The kids learned to be in the room and share space.

They stayed.

Falling up is learning to be in the room no matter what and sharing space with whatever is there to greet you when the eyes close.

Some days, it's like every angel in heaven sings your song. Other days each arduous second scrapes by.

After four months in COVID lockdown, I hadn't done one bit of yoga. My mat lay curled up like a dry leaf. Going back to class, I was a newbie again with newbie fears:

I was for certain the worst in class.

The teacher is inwardly rolling her eyes.

I should give up now.

I want a coffee.

I slunk to the back of the room to uncurl my telltale mat. The class began. After teaching yoga for 35 years, my teacher could see through the walls of my flimsy soul and my flimsier downward dog.

I felt naked, self-conscious and scared, but my goal wasn't for the finest down dog of the day. It was simply to walk through the yoga room door. Just walk in the door. Everything after that was a bonus.

A giggle rippled through the class. We all felt awkward and new returning to the mat after COVID. Like the disillusioned group of city teens, we bonded in our shyness.

The cloud lifted and we were just people on the mat doing that day's downward dog—not tomorrows nor the one we saw on Instagram. Today's.

A mantra taught early and often in my own classes restores even the most doubtful medium to their happy place. That mantra is:

***Stay in the room and keep breathing
(even if you want to leave).***

For yoga lovers it's turning up on the mat greeting whatever today's down dog might be. For mediums, it's arriving to sit with whoever we are today and having that be OK. From that place we share space and invite the spirit world in.

We fall through the open windows of our soul to be caught by the arms of grace.

We rest in a gentle and giant awareness that we are, finally, here in the moment.

When we sit, we drink from a deeper well.

Every minute sitting is a deposit in the soul's bank account and never wasted. No matter what else is going on (and it will be), just turn up and do today's sit.

Not tomorrow's or the glamorous one on Instagram.

Do today's sit and breathe through every minute if you have to.

Everything is waiting for you.

Now it's your turn:

- Remember the gold star stickers from school on good work? Award one every time you sit. Even if it was five minutes.

- Stick them on a progress sheet, then put the sheet on the fridge where all the best work goes.

- Record them in a personal journal.

- Get a medium buddy and check in on each other.

- Wear it on your forehead and wait for comments.

IT MIGHT FEEL LIKE FALLING DOWN INSTEAD OF UP

"God only gives us three answers: yes, no, and I love you too much."

—TOSHA SILVER

Sometimes the answers won't come, no matter how earnestly you stay in the room breathing, waiting to fall up. Some things are tantalisingly out of our reach and 'above our pay grade' to know, and besides, who wants all the answers anyway? It's like opening Christmas presents before Christmas. Part of the magic dies.

If you're a control freak like me, chances are you have a rich history of pre-Christmas present peeking.

Kerry McLeod is a Scottish medium and counsellor who believes that everyone who wants to connect to the spirit world must go within first. We all want to reach that magical spirit place, she says, but good mediumship is a direct byproduct of the work done on the self.

Just as a butterfly is mush inside a cocoon until finally uncrumpling its wings in the sun, so do we undergo major transformations in the practice of falling up. We can feel reduced to mush too. It can feel more like falling down instead of up, and in those times, coming to sit in the stillness of yourself is the hardest challenge.

We find ourselves in the abyss crossed by the Tarot's High Priestess and by Frodo in the Lord of the Rings. It's a heroic inner journey where the beauty of our wings aren't yet on display and all the trust we ever had is asked of us yet again. In short—sitting in the stillness will suck.

When sitting sucks, (and it will) the good news that it will only suck for a short time. Can you sit still like a pond of water till the *suckiness* subsides?

There will be a temptation to run, to move away from pain and toward other answers. Use the energy of the High Priestess of the tarot. She sits between the pillars of heaven and hell because she's been to both. She sits tight, knowing everything has its season. She sits and breathes because she knows there is a divine timing that listens to no one, She knows that this too, shall pass.

When it sucks and the answers don't come, tap into the High Priestess and sit tight. You are going somewhere sacred. The answers are there all along. Just get quiet and listen.

Now it's your turn:

- *Keep sitting.*

- *Keep breathing.*

- *Sit your way through it and wait.*

- *If it's really tough, it might be that our soul has entered the blacksmith's fire and we are forged anew.*

- *In the meantime, stay in the room and sit.*

- *Most people abandon the practice at this point. Don't be one of them. And if you do, forgive yourself and return.*

- *Promise yourself a reward for sitting, even for five minutes. It could be a cup of French Earl Grey in your favourite cup, a gold star, a ten-minute goof off on Pinterest, or a nap.*

ONE-MINUTE WAYS TO FALL UP

"Put down the weight of your aloneness and ease into the conversation. The kettle is singing even as it pours you a drink. The cooking pots have left their arrogant aloofness and seen the good in you at last. All the birds and creatures of the world are unutterably themselves. Everything is waiting for you."

—DAVID WHYTE

The Dalai Lama was asked how an everyday person could be more spiritual, and the expected answer might have been about long hours of cross-legged meditation, mantras, and deprivation. But it wasn't. His startling response was:

Be kind.

That's it.

When we fall up, we move to the universe's big tune, whirling around on daddy's shoes as he dances us around the living room. We are part of the pain and part of the beauty too.

Feeling deeply, we allow ourselves to be danced and to slide into the trainers of another and feel their steps too.

Be kind. Be kind to yourself first—especially with mediumship.

Comparing your insides to someone else's outsides is not kind. You're on track and on time. You have an appointment with your own soul, and it's impossible to be late. Don't let other people dictate the way your spiritual path unfolds because it's yours, it's divine, and it's going marvellously to plan.

Everyone's mediumship arrives at the perfect pace. Loosening the grip on this world to feel the next brings an acceptance of divine timing where we let go of the checklist, to-do pad, and vision board to work with a bigger plan.

Your mediumship is a delicate cocktail of the wondrous soul ability inside and the massive snoozing potential about to be awakened by falling up.

One-minute ways to fall up:

- *Smile at the neighbours.*
- *Make eye contact in the street.*
- *Learn the name of the waitstaff at your local cafe.*
- *Give spare change to the homeless.*
- *Sign petitions to meaningful things.*
- *Offer your seat on public transport.*
- *Listen with your eyes.*

- *Leave water out for dogs and birds on hot days.*

- *Thank your partner/loved ones for the small services they do every day.*

WHEN IT REALLY SUCKS

"Grace is the voice that calls us to change and then gives us the power to pull it off."

— Max Lucado

I could never cook rice. Rice and I have never been friends. Becoming a new dog mother to a ten-year-old rescue dog meant replicating the meals she had in the shelter to make a smoother transition into her new world, and that meant cooking rice for her veggies.

Googling how to cook rice looked ridiculously simple. I gave it a go.

It turned out to be the fluffiest little mountain of white doggie carbs ever. I did a hard (to me) thing.

Cooking rice is a tiny example of doing a hard thing. Maybe you've lived ten lifetimes of hard things. Deaths in the family, sudden severe illnesses, or just the loneliness of being at home, and that's made you mightier too. Maybe you forgot how mighty you are. When we encounter hard things, remember the mightiness of your spirit.

Are there things taken for granted now that you once struggled to do? Make a list on your fingers right now.

Growing spiritually isn't easy, and it's why so many people with mediumship potential and the ability to connect to the unseen world abandon the journey. Travelling the inner distance to meet our own soul seems way too long and scary. But here's the thing: If we don't know our own soul first, how are we going to connect to another and bring a message of healing and love?

Your spiritual season

When it really sucks (congratulations, by the way—big suckage means you're doing it right), one thing that helps is spotting your spiritual season.

Like Melbourne weather, spiritual seasons can happen in one day, one hour, or entire lifetimes. We can cycle through them in a micro moment while still orbiting inside one main season.

We can travel from a frosty winter of inner disappointment to the warmth of the spirit world. Summer could feel full of action and accomplished goals while autumn could rest in quiet journaling afternoons. During a snowbound winter you lie dormant, cocooning, ready to emerge at a better time.

What season might you be in?

Opening to the spirit world as a medium means cracking open the soul first. Choosing to open is a mighty act of spiritual bravery.

Just reading this tiny book is brave. Inside, tiny changes are happening, and soon you'll be ready to open a little more and fall up.

Now it's your turn

Make a list of your mighty acts of bravery. Count them on your fingers right now. Better still, in your journal, or on the fridge. Remind yourself of them when things suck.

A LIST TO HELP YOU KNOW YOU'VE FALLEN UP

"Is this real or just happening inside my head?"

—Harry Potter

It's happening. You're falling up. You've grown in your soul and allowed it to rest in the arms of something greater, however you see that.

Some might say God, or the Universe, Source or Spirit, but it feels different. You are no longer the person you were, even if that moment is brushed briefly along the way.

You've fallen up.

Congratulations.

Here's a tiny list to help you know when it's happened. Can you add more?

- *You feel detached from the small things but oh so connected to the big things.*

- *Your heart bursts often and spills out.*

- *Life seems spacious.*

- *You gaze out the window more often.*

- *You gaze into eyes to see souls.*

- *There is a place for you in the world, and it feels like a good fit.*

- *Things have a habit of turning out OK and even if they don't, it's still OK.*

- *You're not as pushy as you once were.*

- *New friends orbit closer.*

- *Strangers gift random things because your aura is delicious.*

A list to help you know you've fallen up

- *Animals like you even more.*

- *You sometimes touch the majesty of it all and that's enough.*

The spirit world finally moves closer because you've moved closer to your own spirit and can now bring messages through from the unseen world. Most of all, there's a deep soul knowing that you're never alone and always loved. Because you are.

> May you find spirit
> right where
> you are.

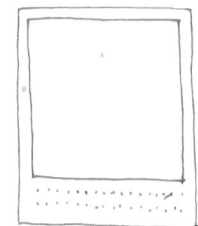

RESOURCES

Falling up needs no props or rituals, just a willingness to sit quietly with no distractions. In the modern world this can be a challenge, and many mediums create recorded audios to help. My two humble offerings are available in the Psychic Classroom:

https://learn.deniselitchfield.com

Hour-long versions created by my favourite mediums Phil Dykes and Kerry McLeod can be found here:

https://thespiritandsoulfoundation.co.uk/mp3-downloads/

The Arthur Findlay College in Stansted, UK, is a residential mediumship training centre fondly known as Hogwarts among its students and Spook Hall by the locals. Explore it here:

https://www.arthurfindlaycollege.org/

Mediumship tutor Paul Jacobs' dedication to mediumship sets the standard for many. Find Paul on Facebook:

https://www.facebook.com/paul.jacobs.1257

ABOUT THE AUTHOR

DENISE LITCHFIELD is a psychic, medium, and author of *Falling up: A guide for nervous mediums.*

She's known for her no BS approach to connecting to the spirit world and wouldn't be caught dead in crushed purple velvet. She doesn't own one crystal.

A self-confessed control freak, Denise is a fan of coffee and journal stickers. She lives with her partner and rescue dog in Sydney's inner west and can be found sipping soy lattes from her vast reusable cup collection.

Find her at:
www.deniselitchfield.com

YouTube:
https://www.youtube.com/c/DeniseLitchfield

www.ingramcontent.com/pod-product-compliance
Lightning Source LLC
Chambersburg PA
CBHW030303010526
44107CB00053B/1806